CROWN CLASSICS

CHRISTINA ROSSETTI
SELECTED POEMS

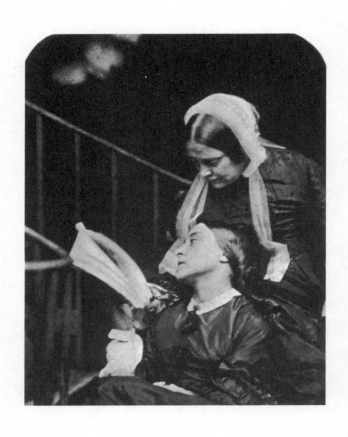

CROWN CLASSICS

Christina Rossetti

Selected Poems

Selected and introduced by
Anthony Eyre

MOUNT ORLEANS
PRESS

Crown Classics Poetry Series
Series editor: Louise Guinness

This collection first published in 2019 by
Mount Orleans Press
23 High Street, Cricklade SN6 6AP
https://anthonyeyre.com

CIP data for this title are available from the British Library

Typography and book production by Anthony Eyre

ISBN 978-1-912945-10-8

Printed in Italy
by Esperia, Lavis (TN)

Frontispiece: Christina Rossetti (seated) with her
mother, photographed by Lewis Carrol

CONTENTS

INTRODUCTION

ON 29 JUNE 1861 Elizabeth Barrett Browning died in Florence. The following year Christina Rossetti, aged 32, published her first collection of poems to be sold commercially, *Goblin Market and Other Poems*. The timing was significant, pregnant with expectation. For many Rossetti was the one to fill the place of the hugely popular Browning; and so it was to prove, Rossetti enjoying a success just as great if not greater. The comparison with Browning was always present. Rossetti herself, in her preface to her sonnet cycle 'Monna Innominata', compared her work to Browning's 'Sonnets from the Portuguese'. By the time she wrote her fourth collection of poems, *A Pageant and Other Poems* (1881), her publisher Alexander Macmillan agreed to print without even having seen the manuscript. Rossetti's place as successor to Browning was universally accepted.

Christina was born in London on 8 December 1830. The Rossetti's were Italian political exiles. Gabriele Rossetti, Christina's father, was a poet who was forced into exile from the Kingdom of the Two Sicilies for his reforming political views. He settled in London in 1824. He took up teaching and was a Professor of Italian at Kings College. His political views are apparent in his naming his eldest son 'Gabriel Charles Dante': the poet Dante was an icon of Italian nationalism and the *Risorgimento*.

Christina's mother was Frances Polidori, herself the

daughter of another Italian, Gaetano Polidori. Gaetano had come to England aged 27 in 1790 and married Anna Maria Pierce, an English governess from Middlesex. Frances grew up in a large household with three sisters and four brothers. Her father Gaetano supported himself by teaching and translating, notably Milton's *Paradise Lost*. He also set up his own private press, where amongst other things he printed the early poems of his grandchildren Dante Gabriel and Christina Rossetti. One of Frances's brothers, Christina's uncle John William Polidori, was physician to Byron, travelling with the poet through Europe to Italy. John also wrote the first vampire novel in English literature, *The Vampyre*, 1819.

Thus the Polidori/Rossetti household in which Christina grew up was strongly Italian in background, with an erudite culture of education and literature. She was the youngest of four children. Both her siblings Maria and William were writers. Her remaining brother, Gabriel Charles Dante but commonly known as Dante Gabriel, was an artist, a leader in the Pre-Raphaelite movement. Dante Gabriel painted and William wrote the manifesto of this movement: a return to simplicity and sincerity, seeking the expression of fundamental truths by focussing on brightly lit detail. In many ways Christina's poetry reflected this aesthetic. The pictorial description in her poems is notable, for example the bedroom scene she creates in 'After Death'. Her poetry, particularly in contrast to Elizabeth Barrett Browning's, is direct and simple, sometimes playfully so:

> ...who ever shows
> His nose to Russian snows
> To be pecked at by every wind that blows?

Sometimes the simplicity will grate: Eric Griffiths ('The Disappointment of Christina G Rossetti', *Essays in Criticism Vol XLVII, No. 2*, OUP 1997) savaged the opening line of her poem 'Golden Glories', 'The buttercup is like a golden cup' — 'Of course it is, otherwise the flower would be called something else — "butterelectricshaver" or "butterfrisbee"'. Another critic at another time, Sir Walter Raleigh at the beginning of the 20th century, commented on how he couldn't read Rossetti without crying. Perhaps the 20th century, with its two World Wars, was not suited to such emotions. The simplicity and the sentiment lie at the heart of the Pre-Raphaelite qualities in Rossetti's poetry.

An essential part of these qualities are rooted in Rossetti's deep Christian faith. This she shared with her family: her sister Maria became a nun. Christina remained single throughout her life, turning down three suitors, one of them, the Pre-Raphaelite artist James Collinson, on the grounds that as an Anglican she could not marry a Catholic. It may seem curious that the Italian Rossettis were Anglicans, but the temporal power of the papacy was seen as one of the major reactionary obstacles to the dream of Italian reunification. Anglicanism would have seemed to them as the purer and less sullied option.

Christina's faith weaves through her poetry. The movement of the seasons becomes a reflection of our faith in and hopes for the future. The bleak mid-winter is the moment for the revelation of our Saviour, with all the hopes of the seasons to come. Earthly love thirsts for divine love — 'Now the Everlasting Arms surround thee,' — and ultimately we reach the hoped for end, 'Sleeping at last in a dreamless sleep locked fast'.

Christina Rossetti died on 29 December 1894, shortly after her 64th birthday. Again like Elizabeth Barrett Browning, she was never healthy, and lived the life of an invalid. She was prolific in her writing, producing over 1,000 poems. She published three major collections: *Goblin Market and Other Poems* (1862); *The Prince's Progress and Other Poems* (1866); and *A Pageant and Other Poems* (1881). There were also volumes of nursery rhymes (*Sing-Song: A Nursery Rhyme Book*, 1872), and religious verse

(*Verses*, 1893); and various works of both fiction and non-fiction, the two religious works *Time Flies: Reading Diary* (1885) and *The Face of the Deep* (1893) being the most famous.

This collection is of necessity a small selection from Rossetti's great *oeuvre*. There is not space to include some of her big narrative poems, for example one of her favourites, 'Goblin Market'; it is in print elsewhere. The selection concentrates on Rossetti's shorter poems and by and large is arranged chronologically.

IN THE ROUND TOWER AT JHANSI
June 8, 1857

A hundred, a thousand to one; even so;
Not a hope in the world remained:
The swarming howling wretches below
Gained and gained and gained.

Skene looked at his pale young wife:—
'Is the time come?' — 'The time is come!' —
Young, strong, and so full of life:
The agony struck them dumb.

Close his arm about her now,
Close her cheek to his,
Close the pistol to her brow —
God forgive them this!

'Will it hurt much?' — 'No, mine own:
I wish I could bear the pang for both.'
'I wish I could bear the pang alone:
Courage, dear, I am not loth.'

Kiss and kiss: 'It is not pain
Thus to kiss and die.
One kiss more.' — 'And yet one again.' —
'Good-bye.' — 'Good-bye.'

AFTER DEATH

The curtains were half drawn, the floor was swept
And strewn with rushes, rosemary and may
Lay thick upon the bed on which I lay,
Where through the lattice ivy-shadows crept.
He leaned above me, thinking that I slept
And could not hear him; but I heard him say:
'Poor child, poor child:' and as he turned away
Came a deep silence, and I knew he wept.
He did not touch the shroud, or raise the fold
That hid my face, or take my hand in his,
Or ruffle the smooth pillows for my head:
He did not love me living; but once dead
He pitied me; and very sweet it is
To know he still is warm though I am cold.

AMOR MUNDI

'Oh where are you going with your love-locks flowing
    On the west wind blowing along this valley track?'
'The downhill path is easy, come with me an it please ye,
    We shall escape the uphill by never turning back.'

So they two went together in glowing August weather,
    The honey-breathing heather lay to their left and right;
And dear she was to dote on,
            her swift feet seemed to float on
    The air like soft twin pigeons too sportive to alight.

'Oh what is that in heaven
            where gray cloud-flakes are seven,
    Where blackest clouds hang riven just at the rainy skirt?'
'Oh that's a meteor sent us, a message dumb, portentous,
    An undeciphered solemn signal of help or hurt.'

'Oh what is that glides quickly
    where velvet flowers grow thickly,
  Their scent comes rich and sickly?'—
    'A scaled and hooded worm.'
'Oh what's that in the hollow, so pale I quake to follow?'
  'Oh that's a thin dead body which waits the eternal term.'

'Turn again, O my sweetest,—turn again, false and fleetest:
  This beaten way thou beatest I fear is hell's own track.'
'Nay, too steep for hill-mounting; nay,
    too late for cost-counting:
  This downhill path is easy, but there's no turning back.'

UP-HILL

Does the road wind up-hill all the way?
Yes, to the very end.
Will the day's journey take the whole long day?
From morn to night, my friend.

But is there for the night a resting-place?
A roof for when the slow dark hours begin.
May not the darkness hide it from my face?
You cannot miss that inn.

Shall I meet other wayfarers at night?
Those who have gone before.
Then must I knock, or call when just in sight?
They will not keep you standing at that door.

Shall I find comfort, travel-sore and weak?
Of labour you shall find the sum.
Will there be beds for me and all who seek?
Yea, beds for all who come.

DREAM LAND

Where sunless rivers weep
Their waves into the deep,
She sleeps a charmèd sleep:
Awake her not.
Led by a single star,
She came from very far
To seek where shadows are
Her pleasant lot.

She left the rosy morn,
She left the fields of corn,
For twilight cold and lorn
And water springs.
Through sleep, as through a veil,
She sees the sky look pale,
And hears the nightingale
That sadly sings.

Rest, rest, a perfect rest
Shed over brow and breast;
Her face is toward the west,
The purple land.
She cannot see the grain
Ripening on hill and plain;
She cannot feel the rain
Upon her hand.

Rest, rest, for evermore
Upon a mossy shore;
Rest, rest at the heart's core
Till time shall cease:
Sleep that no pain shall wake;
Night that no morn shall break
Till joy shall overtake
Her perfect peace.

A BETTER RESURRECTION

I have no wit, no words, no tears;
My heart within me like a stone
Is numbed too much for hopes or fears.
Look right, look left, I dwell alone;
I lift mine eyes, but dimmed with grief
No everlasting hills I see;
My life is in the falling leaf:
O Jesus, quicken me.

My life is like a faded leaf,
My harvest dwindled to a husk;
Truly my life is void and brief
And tedious in the barren dusk;
My life is like a frozen thing,
No bud nor greenness can I see:
Yet rise it shall — the sap of Spring;
O Jesus, rise in me.

My life is like a broken bowl,
A broken bowl that cannot hold
One drop of water for my soul
Or cordial in the searching cold
Cast in the fire the perished thing,
Melt and remould it, till it be
A royal cup for Him my King:
O Jesus, drink of me.

REMEMBER

Sonnet

Remember me when I am gone away,
Gone far away into the silent land;
When you can no more hold me by the hand,
Nor I half turn to go yet turning stay.
Remember me when no more day by day
You tell me of our future that you planned:
Only remember me; you understand
It will be late to counsel then or pray.
Yet if you should forget me for a while
And afterwards remember, do not grieve:
For if the darkness and corruption leave
A vestige of the thoughts that once I had,
Better by far you should forget and smile
Than that you should remember and be sad.

'NO, THANK YOU, JOHN'

I never said I loved you, John:
Why will you tease me day by day,
And wax a weariness to think upon
With always 'do' and 'pray'?

You know I never loved you, John;
No fault of mine made me your toast:
Why will you haunt me with a face as wan
As shows an hour-old ghost?

I dare say Meg or Moll would take
Pity upon you, if you'd ask:
And pray don't remain single for my sake
Who can't perform that task.

I have no heart? — Perhaps I have not;
But then you're mad to take offence
That I don't give you what I have not got:
Use your own common sense.

Let bygones be bygones:
Don't call me false, who owed not to be true:
I'd rather answer 'No' to fifty Johns
Than answer 'Yes' to you.

Let's mar our pleasant days no more,
Song-birds of passage, days of youth:
Catch at today, forget the days before:
I'll wink at your untruth.

Let us strike hands as hearty friends;
No more, no less; and friendship's good:
Only don't keep in view ulterior ends,
And points not understood

In open treaty. Rise above
Quibbles and shuffling off and on:
Here's friendship for you if
you like; but love, —
No, thank you, John.

CHRISTINA ROSSETTI

A BIRTHDAY

My heart is like a singing bird
   Whose nest is in a water'd shoot;
My heart is like an apple-tree
   Whose boughs are bent with thick-set fruit;
My heart is like a rainbow shell
   That paddles in a halcyon sea;
My heart is gladder than all these,
   Because my love is come to me.

Raise me a daïs of silk and down;
   Hang it with vair and purple dyes;
Carve it in doves and pomegranates,
   And peacocks with a hundred eyes;
Work it in gold and silver grapes,
   In leaves and silver fleurs-de-lys;
Because the birthday of my life
   Is come, my love is come to me.

WIFE TO HUSBAND

Pardon the faults in me,
For the love of years ago:
Good-bye.
I must drift across the sea,
I must sink into the snow,
I must die.

You can bask in this sun,
You can drink wine, and eat:
Good-bye.
I must gird myself and run,
Though with unready feet:
I must die.

Blank sea to sail upon,
Cold bed to sleep in:
Good-bye.
While you clasp, I must be gone
For all your weeping:
I must die.

A kiss for one friend,
And a word for two, —
Good-bye: —
A lock that you must send,
A kindness you must do:
I must die.

Not a word for you,
Not a lock or kiss,
Good-bye.
We, one, must part in two;
Verily death is this:
I must die.

ECHO

Come to me in the silence of the night;
Come in the speaking silence of a dream;
Come with soft rounded cheeks and eyes as bright
As sunlight on a stream;
Come back in tears,
O memory, hope, love of finished years.

O dream how sweet, too sweet, too bitter sweet,
Whose wakening should have been in Paradise,
Where souls brimful of love abide and meet;
Where thirsting longing eyes
Watch the slow door
That opening, letting in, lets out no more.

Yet come to me in dreams, that I may live
My very life again though cold in death:
Come back to me in dreams, that I may give
Pulse for pulse, breath for breath:
Speak low, lean low,
As long ago, my love, how long ago!

COUSIN KATE

I was a cottage maiden
Hardened by sun and air,
Contented with my cottage mates,
Not mindful I was fair.
Why did a great lord find me out,
And praise my flaxen hair?
Why did a great lord find me out
To fill my heart with care?

He lured me to his palace home —
Woe's me for joy thereof —
To lead a shameless shameful life,
His plaything and his love.
He wore me like a silken knot,
He changed me like a glove;
So now I moan, an unclean thing,
Who might have been a dove.

O Lady Kate, my cousin Kate,
You grew more fair than I:
He saw you at your father's gate,
Chose you, and cast me by.
He watched your steps along the lane,
Your work among the rye;
He lifted you from mean estate
To sit with him on high.

Because you were so good and pure
He bound you with his ring:
The neighbours call you good and pure,
Call me an outcast thing.
Even so I sit and howl in dust,
You sit in gold and sing:
Now which of us has tenderer heart?
You had the stronger wing.

O cousin Kate, my love was true,
Your love was writ in sand:
If he had fooled not me but you,
If you stood where I stand,
He'd not have won me with his love
Nor bought me with his land;
I would have spit into his face
And not have taken his hand.

Yet I've a gift you have not got,
And seem not like to get:
For all your clothes and wedding-ring
I've little doubt you fret.
My fair-haired son, my shame, my pride,
Cling closer, closer yet:
Your father would give lands for one
To wear his coronet.

THE CONVENT THRESHOLD

There's blood between us, love, my love,
There's father's blood, there's brother's blood;
And blood's a bar I cannot pass:
I choose the stairs that mount above,
Stair after golden skyward stair,
To city and to sea of glass.
My lily feet are soiled with mud,
With scarlet mud which tells a tale
Of hope that was, of guilt that was,
Of love that shall not yet avail;
Alas, my heart, if I could bare
My heart, this selfsame stain is there:
I seek the sea of glass and fire
To wash the spot, to burn the snare;
Lo, stairs are meant to lift us higher:
Mount with me, mount the kindled stair.

Your eyes look earthward, mine look up.
I see the far-off city grand,
Beyond the hills a watered land,
Beyond the gulf a gleaming strand
Of mansions where the righteous sup;
Who sleep at ease among their trees,
Or wake to sing a cadenced hymn
With Cherubim and Seraphim;
They bore the Cross, they drained the cup,
Racked, roasted, crushed,
wrenched limb from limb,
They the offscouring of the world:
The heaven of starry heavens unfurled,
The sun before their face is dim.

You looking earthward what see you?
Milk-white wine-flushed among the vines,
Up and down leaping, to and fro,
Most glad, most full, made strong with wines,

Blooming as peaches pearled with dew,
Their golden windy hair afloat,
Love-music warbling in their throat,
Young men and women come and go.

You linger, yet the time is short:
Flee for your life, gird up your strength
To flee; the shadows stretched at length
Show that day wanes, that night draws nigh;
Flee to the mountain, tarry not.
Is this a time for smile and sigh,
For songs among the secret trees
Where sudden blue birds nest and sport?
The time is short and yet you stay:
To-day while it is called today
Kneel, wrestle, knock, do violence, pray;
To-day is short, tomorrow nigh:
Why will you die? why will you die?

You sinned with me a pleasant sin:
Repent with me, for I repent.
Woe's me the lore I must unlearn!
Woe's me that easy way we went,
So rugged when I would return!
How long until my sleep begin,
How long shall stretch these nights and days?
Surely, clean Angels cry, she prays;
She laves her soul with tedious tears:
How long must stretch these years and years?

I turn from you my cheeks and eyes,
My hair which you shall see no more —
Alas for joy that went before,
For joy that dies, for love that dies.
Only my lips still turn to you,
My livid lips that cry, Repent.
Oh weary life, oh weary Lent,
Oh weary time whose stars are few.

How should I rest in Paradise,
Or sit on steps of heaven alone?
If Saints and Angels spoke of love
Should I not answer from my throne:
Have pity upon me, ye my friends,
For I have heard the sound thereof:
Should I not turn with yearning eyes,
Turn earthwards with a pitiful pang?
Oh save me from a pang in heaven.
By all the gifts we took and gave,
Repent, repent, and be forgiven:
This life is long, but yet it ends;
Repent and purge your soul and save:
No gladder song the morning stars
Upon their birthday morning sang
Than Angels sing when one repents.

I tell you what I dreamed last night:
A spirit with transfigured face
Fire-footed clomb an infinite space.
I heard his hundred pinions clang,
Heaven-bells rejoicing rang and rang,
Heaven-air was thrilled with subtle scents,
Worlds spun upon their rushing cars:
He mounted shrieking: 'Give me light.'
Still light was poured on him, more light;
Angels, Archangels he outstripped
Exultant in exceeding might,
And trod the skirts of Cherubim.
Still 'Give me light,' he shrieked; and dipped
His thirsty face, and drank a sea,
Athirst with thirst it could not slake.
I saw him, drunk with knowledge, take
From aching brows the aureole crown —
His locks writhed like a cloven snake —
He left his throne to grovel down
And lick the dust of Seraphs' feet:

For what is knowledge duly weighed?
Knowledge is strong, but love is sweet;
Yea all the progress he had made
Was but to learn that all is small
Save love, for love is all in all.

I tell you what I dreamed last night:
It was not dark, it was not light,
Cold dews had drenched my plenteous hair
Through clay; you came to seek me there.
And 'Do you dream of me?' you said.
My heart was dust that used to leap
To you; I answered half asleep:
'My pillow is damp, my sheets are red,
There's a leaden tester to my bed:
Find you a warmer playfellow,
A warmer pillow for your head,
A kinder love to love than mine.'
You wrung your hands; while I like lead
Crushed downwards through the sodden earth:
You smote your hands but not in mirth,
And reeled but were not drunk with wine.

For all night long I dreamed of you:
I woke and prayed against my will,
Then slept to dream of you again.
At length I rose and knelt and prayed:
I cannot write the words I said,
My words were slow, my tears were few;
But through the dark my silence spoke
Like thunder. When this morning broke,
My face was pinched, my hair was grey,
And frozen blood was on the sill
Where stifling in my struggle I lay.

If now you saw me you would say:
Where is the face I used to love?
And I would answer: Gone before;

It tarries veiled in paradise.
When once the morning star shall rise,
When earth with shadow flees away
And we stand safe within the door,
Then you shall lift the veil thereof.
Look up, rise up: for far above
Our palms are grown, our place is set;
There we shall meet as once we met
And love with old familiar love.

MAUDE CLARE

Out of the church she followed them
With a lofty step and mien:
His bride was like a village maid,
Maude Clare was like a queen.

'Son Thomas,' his lady mother said,
With smiles, almost with tears:
'May Nell and you but live as true
As we have done for years;

'Your father thirty years ago
Had just your tale to tell;
But he was not so pale as you,
Nor I so pale as Nell.'

My lord was pale with inward strife,
And Nell was pale with pride;
My lord gazed long on pale Maude Clare
Or ever he kissed the bride.

'Lo, I have brought my gift, my lord,
Have brought my gift,' she said:
'To bless the hearth, to bless the board,
To bless the marriage-bed.

'Here's my half of the golden chain
You wore about your neck,
That day we waded ankle-deep
For lilies in the beck:

'Here's my half of the faded leaves
We plucked from budding bough,
With feet amongst the lily leaves, —
The lilies are budding now.'

He strove to match her scorn with scorn,
He faltered in his place:
'Lady,' he said, — 'Maude Clare,' he said, —
'Maude Clare:' — and hid his face.

She turn'd to Nell: 'My Lady Nell,
I have a gift for you;
Though, were it fruit, the bloom were gone,
Or, were it flowers, the dew.

'Take my share of a fickle heart,
Mine of a paltry love:
Take it or leave it as you will,
I wash my hands thereof.'

'And what you leave,' said Nell, 'I'll take,
And what you spurn, I'll wear;
For he's my lord for better and worse,
And him I love, Maude Clare.

'Yea, though you're taller by the head,
More wise, and much more fair;
I'll love him till he loves me best,
Me best of all, Maude Clare.'

A TRIAD

Three sang of love together: one with lips
   Crimson, with cheeks and bosom in a glow,
Flushed to the yellow hair and finger tips;
   And one there sang who soft and smooth as snow
   Bloomed like a tinted hyacinth at a show;
And one was blue with famine after love,
   Who like a harpstring snapped rang harsh and low
The burden of what those were singing of.
One shamed herself in love; one temperately
   Grew gross in soulless love, a sluggish wife;
One famished died for love. Thus two of three
   Took death for love and won him after strife;
One droned in sweetness like a fattened bee:
   All on the threshold, yet all short of life.

THE THREE ENEMIES

The Flesh

'Sweet, thou art pale.'
'More pale to see,
Christ hung upon the cruel tree
And bore His Father's wrath for me.'

'Sweet, thou art sad.'
'Beneath a rod
More heavy, Christ for my sake trod
The winepress of the wrath of God.'

'Sweet, thou art weary.'
'Not so Christ:
Whose mighty love of me sufficed
For Strength, Salvation, Eucharist.'

'Sweet, thou art footsore.'
'If I bleed,
His feet have bled; yea in my need
His Heart once bled for mine indeed.'

The World

'Sweet, thou art young.'
'So He was young
Who for my sake in silence hung
Upon the Cross with Passion wrung.'

'Look, thou art fair.'
'He was more fair
Than men, Who deigned for me to wear
A visage marred beyond compare.'

'And thou hast riches.'
'Daily bread:
All else is His: Who, living, dead,
For me lacked where to lay His Head.'

'And life is sweet.'
'It was not so
To Him, Whose Cup did overflow
With mine unutterable woe.'

The Devil

'Thou drinkest deep.'
'When Christ would sup
He drained the dregs from out my cup:
So how should I be lifted up?'

'Thou shalt win Glory.'
'In the skies,
Lord Jesus, cover up mine eyes
Lest they should look on vanities.'

'Thou shalt have Knowledge.'
'Helpless dust!
In Thee, O Lord, I put my trust:
Answer Thou for me, Wise and Just.'

'And Might.' —
'Get thee behind me. Lord,
Who hast redeemed and not abhorred
My soul, oh keep it by Thy Word.'

SONG (1862)

When I am dead, my dearest,
    Sing no sad songs for me;
Plant thou no roses at my head,
    Nor shady cypress tree:
Be the green grass above me
    With showers and dewdrops wet:
And if thou wilt, remember,
    And if thou wilt, forget.

I shall not see the shadows,
    I shall not feel the rain;
I shall not hear the nightingale
    Sing on as if in pain:
And dreaming through the twilight
    That doth not rise nor set,
Haply I may remember,
    And haply may forget.

A PORTRAIT

I

She gave up beauty in her tender youth,
  Gave all her hope and joy and pleasant ways;
  She covered up her eyes lest they should gaze
On vanity, and chose the bitter truth.
Harsh towards herself, towards others full of ruth,
  Servant of servants, little known to praise,
  Long prayers and fasts trenched on her nights and days:
She schooled herself to sights and sounds uncouth
That with the poor and stricken she might make
  A home, until the least of all sufficed
Her wants; her own self learned she to forsake,
Counting all earthly gain but hurt and loss.
So with calm will she chose and bore the cross
  And hated all for love of Jesus Christ.

II

They knelt in silent anguish by her bed,
  And could not weep; but calmly there she lay.
  All pain had left her; and the sun's last ray
Shone through upon her, warming into red
The shady curtains. In her heart she said:
  'Heaven opens; I leave these and go away;
  The Bridegroom calls, — shall the Bride seek to stay?'
Then low upon her breast she bowed her head.
O lily flower, O gem of priceless worth,
  O dove with patient voice and patient eyes,
O fruitful vine amid a land of dearth,
  O maid replete with loving purities,
Thou bowedst down thy head with friends on earth
  To raise it with the saints in Paradise.

TWICE

I took my heart in my hand
  (O my love, O my love),
I said: Let me fall or stand,
  Let me live or die,
But this once hear me speak —
  (O my love, O my love) —
Yet a woman's words are weak;
  You should speak, not I.

You took my heart in your hand
  With a friendly smile,
With a critical eye you scanned,
  Then set it down,
And said: It is still unripe,
  Better wait awhile;
Wait while the skylarks pipe,
  Till the corn grows brown.

As you set it down it broke —
  Broke, but I did not wince;
I smiled at the speech you spoke,
  At your judgement that I heard:
But I have not often smiled
  Since then, nor questioned since,
Nor cared for corn-flowers wild,
  Nor sung with the singing bird.

I take my heart in my hand,
  O my God, O my God,
My broken heart in my hand:
  Thou hast seen, judge Thou.
My hope was written on sand,
  O my God, O my God:
Now let thy judgement stand —
  Yea, judge me now.

This contemned of a man,
  This marred one heedless day,
This heart take Thou to scan
  Both within and without:
Refine with fire its gold,
  Purge thou its dross away —
Yea, hold it in Thy hold,
  Whence none can pluck it out.

I take my heart in my hand —
  I shall not die, but live —
Before Thy face I stand;
  I, for Thou callest such:
All that I have I bring,
  All that I am I give,
Smile Thou and I shall sing,
  But shall not question much.

THE QUEEN OF HEARTS

How comes it, Flora, that, whenever we
Play cards together, you invariably,
  However the pack parts,
  Still hold the Queen of Hearts?

I've scanned you with a scrutinizing gaze,
Resolved to fathom these your secret ways:
  But, sift them as I will,
  Your ways are secret still.

I cut and shuffle; shuffle, cut, again;
But all my cutting, shuffling, proves in vain:
  Vain hope, vain forethought too;
  The Queen still falls to you.

I dropped her once, prepense; but, ere the deal
Was dealt, your instinct seemed her loss to feel:
   'There should be one card more,'
   You said, and searched the floor.

I cheated once; I made a private notch
In Heart–Queen's back, and
kept a lynx-eyed watch;
   Yet such another back
   Deceived me in the pack:

The Queen of Clubs assumed by arts unknown
An imitative dint that seemed my own;
   This notch, not of my doing,
   Misled me to my ruin.

It baffles me to puzzle out the clue,
Which must be skill, or craft, or luck in you:
   Unless, indeed, it be
   Natural affinity.

A RING POSY

   Jess and Jill are pretty girls,
     Plump and well to do,
   In a cloud of windy curls:
     Yet I know who
   Loves me more than curls or pearls.

   I'm not pretty, not a bit —
     Thin and sallow-pale;
   When I trudge along the street
     I don't need a veil:
   Yet I have one fancy hit.

Jess and Jill can trill and sing
  With a flute-like voice,
Dance as light as bird on wing,
  Laugh for careless joys:
Yet it's I who wear the ring.

Jess and Jill will mate some day,
  Surely, surely:
Ripen on to June through May,
While the sun shines make their hay,
  Slacken steps demurely:
Yet even there I lead the way.

LADY MAGGIE

You must not call me Maggie, you must not call me Dear,
  For I'm Lady of the Manor now stately to see;
And if there comes a babe, as there may some happy year,
  'Twill be little lord or lady at my knee.

Oh, but what ails you, my sailor cousin Phil,
  That you shake and turn white like a cockcrow ghost?
You're as white as I turned once down by the mill,
  When one told me you and ship and crew were lost:

Philip my playfellow, when we were boy and girl
  (It was the Miller's Nancy told it to me),
Philip with the merry life in lip and curl,
  Philip my playfellow drowned in the sea!

I thought I should have fainted, but I did not faint;
  I stood stunned at the moment, scarcely sad,
Till I raised my wail of desolate complaint
  For you, my cousin, brother, all I had.

They said I looked so pale — some say so fair —
  My lord stopped in passing to soothe me back to life:
I know I missed a ringlet from my hair
  Next morning; and now I am his wife.

Look at my gown, Philip, and look at my ring,
  I'm all crimson and gold from top to toe:
All day long I sit in the sun and sing,
  Where in the sun red roses blush and blow.

And I'm the rose of roses says my lord;
  And to him I'm more than the sun in the sky,
While I hold him fast with the golden cord
  Of a curl, with the eyelash of an eye.

His mother said 'fie,' and his sisters cried 'shame,'
  His highborn ladies cried 'shame' from their place:
They said 'fie' when they only heard my name,
  But fell silent when they saw my face.

Am I so fair, Philip? Philip, did you think
  I was so fair when we played boy and girl,
Where blue forget-me-nots bloomed on the brink
  Of our stream which the mill-wheel sent a whirl?

If I was fair then sure I'm fairer now,
  Sitting where a score of servants stand,
With a coronet on high days for my brow
  And almost a sceptre for my hand.

You're but a sailor, Philip, weatherbeaten brown,
  A stranger on land and at home on the sea,
Coasting as best you may from town to town:
  Coasting along do you often think of me?

I'm a great lady in a sheltered bower,
  With hands grown white through having nought to do:
Yet sometimes I think of you hour after hour
  Till I nigh wish myself a child with you.

WHAT WOULD I GIVE?

What would I give for a heart of flesh to warm me through,
Instead of this heart of stone ice-cold whatever I do;
Hard and cold and small, of all hearts the worst of all.

What would I give for words, if only words would come;
But now in its misery my spirit has fallen dumb:
Oh, merry friends, go your own way,
    I have never a word to say.

What would I give for tears, not smiles but scalding tears,
To wash the black mark clean, and
    to thaw the frost of years,
To wash the stain ingrain and to make me clean again.

MEMORY

I

I nursed it in my bosom while it lived,
  I hid it in my heart when it was dead;
In joy I sat alone, even so I grieved
    Alone and nothing said.

I shut the door to face the naked truth,
  I stood alone — I faced the truth alone,
Stripped bare of self-regard or forms or ruth
    Till first and last were shown.

I took the perfect balances and weighed;
  No shaking of my hand disturbed the poise;
Weighed, found it wanting: not a word I said,
    But silent made my choice.

None know the choice I made; I make it still.
  None know the choice I made and broke my heart,
Breaking mine idol: I have braced my will
    Once, chosen for once my part.

I broke it at a blow, I laid it cold,
  Crushed in my deep heart where it used to live.
My heart dies inch by inch; the time grows old,
    Grows old in which I grieve.

II

I have a room whereinto no one enters
  Save I myself alone:
  There sits a blessed memory on a throne,
There my life centres.

While winter comes and goes – oh tedious comer! –
  And while its nip-wind blows;
  While bloom the bloodless lily and warm rose
Of lavish summer.

If any should force entrance he might see there
  One buried yet not dead,
  Before whose face I no more bow my head
Or bend my knee there;

But often in my worn life's autumn weather
  I watch there with clear eyes,
  And think how it will be in Paradise
When we're together.

SHALL I FORGET?

Shall I forget on this side of the grave?
I promise nothing: you must wait and see
    Patient and brave.
(O my soul, watch with him and he with me.)

Shall I forget in peace of Paradise?
I promise nothing: follow, friend, and see
    Faithful and wise.
(O my soul, lead the way he walks with me.)

A FARM WALK

The year stood at its equinox
    And bluff the North was blowing,
A bleat of lambs came from the flocks,
    Green hardy things were growing;
I met a maid with shining locks
    Where milky kine were lowing.

She wore a kerchief on her neck,
    Her bare arm showed its dimple,
Her apron spread without a speck,
    Her air was frank and simple.

She milked into a wooden pail
    And sang a country ditty,
An innocent fond lovers' tale,
    That was not wise nor witty,
Pathetically rustical,
    Too pointless for the city.

She kept in time without a beat
  As true as church-bell ringers,
Unless she tapped time with her feet,
  Or squeezed it with her fingers;
Her clear unstudied notes were sweet
  As many a practised singer's.

I stood a minute out of sight,
  Stood silent for a minute
To eye the pail, and creamy white
  The frothing milk within it;

To eye the comely milking maid
  Herself so fresh and creamy:
'Good day to you,' at last I said;
  She turned her head to see me:
'Good day,' she said with lifted head;
  Her eyes looked soft and dreamy,

And all the while she milked and milked
  The grave cow heavy-laden:
I've seen grand ladies plumed and silked,
  But not a sweeter maiden;

But not a sweeter fresher maid
  Than this in homely cotton,
Whose pleasant face and silky braid
  I have not yet forgotten.

Seven springs have passed since then, as I
  Count with a sober sorrow;
Seven springs have come and passed me by,
  And spring sets in tomorrow.

I've half a mind to shake myself
  Free just for once from London,
To set my work upon the shelf
  And leave it done or undone;

To run down by the early train,
  Whirl down with shriek and whistle,
And feel the bluff North blow again,
  And mark the sprouting thistle
Set up on waste patch of the lane
  Its green and tender bristle.

And spy the scarce-blown violet banks,
  Crisp primrose leaves and others,
And watch the lambs leap at their pranks
  And butt their patient mothers.
Alas, one point in all my plan
  My serious thoughts demur to:
Seven years have passed for maid and man,
  Seven years have passed for her too;

Perhaps my rose is overblown,
  Not rosy or too rosy;
Perhaps in farmhouse of her own
  Some husband keeps her cosy,
Where I should show a face unknown.
  Good-bye, my wayside posy.

SOMEWHERE OR OTHER

Somewhere or other there must surely be
  The face not seen, the voice not heard,
The heart that not yet — never yet — ah me!
  Made answer to my word.

Somewhere or other, may be near or far;
  Past land and sea, clean out of sight;
Beyond the wandering moon, beyond the star
  That tracks her night by night.

Somewhere or other, may be far or near;
  With just a wall, a hedge, between;
With just the last leaves of the dying year
  Fallen on a turf grown green.

CHILD'S TALK IN APRIL

I wish you were a pleasant wren,
  And I your small accepted mate;
How we'd look down on toilsome men!
  We'd rise and go to bed at eight
  Or it may be not quite so late.

Then you should see the nest I'd build,
  The wondrous nest for you and me;
The outside rough perhaps, but filled
  With wool and down; ah, you should see
  The cosy nest that it would be.

We'd have our change of hope and fear,
  Small quarrels, reconcilements sweet:
I'd perch by you to chirp and cheer,
  Or hop about on active feet,
  And fetch you dainty bits to eat.

We'd be so happy by the day,
  So safe and happy through the night,
We both should feel, and I should say,
  It's all one season of delight,
And we'll make merry whilst we may.

Perhaps some day there'd be an egg
  When spring had blossomed from the snow:
I'd stand triumphant on one leg;
  Like chanticleer I'd almost crow
  To let our little neighbours know.

Next you should sit and I would sing
Through lengthening days of sunny spring;
  Till, if you wearied of the task,
I'd sit; and you should spread your wing
  From bough to bough; I'd sit and bask.

Fancy the breaking of the shell,
  The chirp, the chickens wet and bare,
The untried proud paternal swell;
  And you with housewife-matron air
  Enacting choicer bills of fare.

Fancy the embryo coats of down,
  The gradual feathers soft and sleek;
Till clothed and strong from tail to crown,
  With virgin warblings in their beak,
  They too go forth to soar and seek.

So would it last an April through
And early summer fresh with dew:
  Then should we part and live as twain,
Love-time would bring me back to you
  And build our happy nest again.

WINTER: MY SECRET

I tell my secret? No indeed, not I;
Perhaps some day, who knows?
But not today; it froze, and blows and snows,
And you're too curious: fie!
You want to hear it? well:
Only, my secret's mine, and I won't tell.

Or, after all, perhaps there's none:
Suppose there is no secret after all,
But only just my fun.
Today's a nipping day, a biting day;
In which one wants a shawl,
A veil, a cloak, and other wraps:
I cannot ope to everyone who taps,
And let the draughts come
                    whistling thro' my hall;
Come bounding and surrounding me,
Come buffeting, astounding me,
Nipping and clipping thro' my wraps and all.
I wear my mask for warmth: who ever shows
His nose to Russian snows
To be pecked at by every wind that blows?
You would not peck? I thank you for good will,
Believe, but leave the truth untested still.

Spring's an expansive time: yet I don't trust
March with its peck of dust,
Nor April with its rain-
bow-crowned brief showers,
Nor even May, whose flowers
One frost may wither thro' the sunless hours.

Perhaps some languid summer day,
When drowsy birds sing less and less,
And golden fruit is ripening to excess,
If there's not too much sun nor too much cloud,
And the warm wind is neither still nor loud,
Perhaps my secret I may say,
Or you may guess.

WEARY IN WELL-DOING

I would have gone; God bade me stay:
  I would have worked; God bade me rest.
He broke my will from day to day,
  He read my yearnings unexpressed
    And said them nay.

Now I would stay; God bids me go:
  Now I would rest; God bids me work.
He breaks my heart tossed to and fro,
  My soul is wrung with doubts that lurk
    And vex it so.

I go, Lord, where Thou sendest me;
  Day after day I plod and moil:
But, Christ my God, when will it be
  That I may let alone my toil
    And rest with Thee?

IN THE BLEAK MID-WINTER

In the bleak mid-winter
Frosty wind made moan;
Earth stood hard as iron,
Water like a stone;
Snow had fallen, snow on snow,
Snow on snow,
In the bleak mid-winter
Long ago.

Our God, heaven cannot hold Him
Nor earth sustain,
Heaven and earth shall flee away
When He comes to reign:
In the bleak mid-winter
A stable-place sufficed
The Lord God Almighty —
Jesus Christ.

Enough for Him, whom Cherubim
Worship night and day,
A breastful of milk
And a mangerful of hay;
Enough for Him, whom Angels
Fall down before,
The ox and ass and camel
Which adore.

Angels and Archangels
May have gathered there,
Cherubim and seraphim
Thronged the air;
But only His Mother
In her maiden bliss
Worshipped the Beloved
With a kiss.

What can I give Him,
Poor as I am? —
If I were a Shepherd
I would bring a lamb;
If I were a Wise Man
I would do my part, —
Yet what I can I give Him, —
Give my heart.

A BIRD SONG

It's a year almost that I have not seen her:
Oh, last summer green things were greener,
Brambles fewer, the blue sky bluer.

It's surely summer, for there's a swallow:
Come one swallow, his mate will follow,
The bird race quicken and wheel and thicken.

Oh happy swallow whose mate will follow
O'er height, o'er hollow! I'd be a swallow,
To build this weather one nest together.

ONE SWALLOW DOES NOT
MAKE A SUMMER

A rose which spied one swallow
Made haste to blush and blow:
"Others are sure to follow:"
Ah no, not so!
The wandering clouds still owe
A few fresh flakes of snow,
Chill fog must fill the hollow,
Before the bird-stream flow
In flood across the main
And winter's woe
End in glad summer come again.
Then thousand flowers may blossom by the shore,
But that Rose never more.

THE KEY-NOTE

Where are the songs I used to know,
Where are the notes I used to sing?
I have forgotten everything
I used to know so long ago;
Summer has followed after Spring;
Now Autumn is so shrunk and sere,
I scarcely think a sadder thing
Can be the Winter of my year.

Yet Robin sings through Winter's rest,
When bushes put their berries on;
While they their ruddy jewels don,
He sings out of a ruddy breast;
The hips and haws and ruddy breast
Make one spot warm where snowflakes lie
They break and cheer the unlovely rest
Of Winter's pause — and why not I?

PASTIME

A boat amid the ripples, drifting, rocking,
Two idle people, without pause or aim;
While in the ominous west there gathers darkness
Flushed with flame.

A haycock in a hayfield backing, lapping,
Two drowsy people pillowed round about;
While in the ominous west across the darkness
Flame leaps out.

Better a wrecked life than a life so aimless,
Better a wrecked life than a life so soft ;
The ominous west glooms thundering, with its fire
Lit aloft.

"ITALIA, IO TI SALUTO!"

To come back from the sweet South, to the North
Where I was born, bred, look to die;
Come back to do my day's work in its day,
Play out my play—
Amen, amen, say I.

To see no more the country half my own,
Nor hear the half familiar speech,
Amen, I say; I turn to that bleak North
Whence I came forth —
The South lies out of reach.

But when our swallows fly back to the South,
To the sweet South, to the sweet South,
The tears may come again into my eyes
On the old wise,
And the sweet name to my mouth.

YET A LITTLE WHILE

I dreamed and did not seek: to-day I seek
Who can no longer dream;
But now am all behindhand, waxen weak,
And dazed amid so many things that gleam
Yet are not what they seem.

I dreamed and did not work: to-day I work
Kept wide awake by care
And loss, and perils dimly guessed to lurk;
I work and reap not, while my life goes bare
And void in wintry air.

I hope indeed; but hope itself is fear
Viewed on the sunny side;
I hope, and disregard the world that's here,
The prizes drawn, the sweet things that betide;
I hope, and I abide.

HE AND SHE

"Should one of us remember,
And one of us forget,
I wish I knew what each will do —
But who can tell as yet?"

"Should one of us remember,
And one of us forget,
I promise you what I will do —
And I'm content to wait for you,
And not be sure as yet."

DE PROFUNDIS

Oh why is heaven built so far,
Oh why is earth set so remote?
I cannot reach the nearest star
That hangs afloat.

I would not care to reach the moon,
One round monotonous of change;
Yet even she repeats her tune
Beyond my range.

I never watch the scattered fire
Of stars, or sun's far-trailing train,
But all my heart is one desire,
And all in vain:

For I am bound with fleshly bands,
Joy, beauty, lie beyond my scope;
I strain my heart, I stretch my hands,
And catch at hope.

TOUCHING "NEVER"

Because you never yet have loved me, dear,
Think you you never can nor ever will?
Surely while life remains hope lingers still,
Hope the last blossom of life's dying year.
Because the season and mine age grow sere,
Shall never Spring bring forth her daffodil,
Shall never sweeter Summer feast her fill
Of roses with the nightingales they hear?
If you had loved me, I not loving you,
If you had urged me with the tender plea
Of what our unknown years to come might do
(Eternal years, if Time should count too few),
I would have owned the point you pressed on me,
Was possible, or probable, or true.

from MONNA INNOMINATA

I I

I wish I could remember that first day,
First hour, first moment of your meeting me,
If bright or dim the season, it might be
Summer or Winter for aught I can say;
So unrecorded did it slip away,
So blind was I to see and to foresee,
So dull to mark the budding of my tree
That would not blossom yet for many a May.
If only I could recollect it, such
A day of days! I let it come and go
As traceless as a thaw of bygone snow;
It seemed to mean so little, meant so much;
If only now I could recall that touch,
First touch of hand in hand — Did one but know!

I V

I loved you first: but afterwards your love
Outsoaring mine, sang such a loftier song
As drowned the friendly cooings of my dove.
Which owes the other most? my love was long,
And yours one moment seemed to wax more strong;
I loved and guessed at you, you construed me
And loved me for what might or might not be —
Nay, weights and measures do us both a wrong.
For verily love knows not "mine" or " thine;"
With separate "I" and "thou" free love has done,
For one is both and both are one in love:
Rich love knows nought of "thine that is not mine;"
Both have the strength and both the length thereof,
Both of us of the love which makes us one.

JOHNNY

*Founded on an Anecdote of the First French
Revolution*

Johnny had a golden head
Like a golden mop in blow,
Right and left his curls would spread
In a glory and a glow,
And they framed his honest face
Like stray sunbeams out of place.

Long and thick, they half could hide
How threadbare his patched jacket hung;
They used to be his Mother's pride;
She praised them with a tender tongue,
And stroked them with a loving finger
That smoothed and stroked
        and loved to linger.

On a doorstep Johnny sat,
Up and down the street looked he;
Johnny did not own a hat,
Hot or cold tho' days might be;
Johnny did not own a boot
To cover up his muddy foot.

Johnny's face was pale and thin,
Pale with hunger and with crying;
For his Mother lay within,
Talked and tossed and seemed a-dying,
While Johnny racked his brains to think
How to get her help and drink,

Get her physic, get her tea,
Get her bread and something nice;
Not a penny piece had he,
And scarce a shilling might suffice;
No wonder that his soul was sad,
When not one penny piece he had.

As he sat there thinking, moping,
Because his Mother's wants were many,
Wishing much but scarcely hoping
To earn a shilling or a penny,
A friendly neighbour passed him by
And questioned him: Why did he cry?

Alas! his trouble soon was told:
He did not cry for cold or hunger,
Though he was hungry both and cold;
He only felt more weak and younger,
Because he wished so to be old
And apt at earning pence or gold.

Kindly that neighbour was, but poor,
Scant coin had he to give or lend;
And well he guessed there needed more
Than pence or shillings to befriend
The helpless woman in her strait,
So much loved, yet so desolate.

One way he saw, and only one:
He would — he could not — give the advice,
And yet he must: the widow's son

Had curls of gold would fetch their price;
Long curls which might be clipped, and sold
For silver, or perhaps for gold.

Our Johnny, when he understood
Which shop it was that purchased hair,
Ran off as briskly as he could,
And in a trice stood cropped and bare,
Too short of hair to fill a locket,
But jingling money in his pocket.

Precious money — tea and bread,
Physic, ease, for Mother dear,
Better than a golden head:
Yet our hero dropped one tear
When he spied himself close shorn,
Barer much than lamb new born.

His Mother throve upon the money,
Ate and revived and kissed her son:
But oh! when she perceived her Johnny,
And understood what he had done
All and only for her sake,
She sobbed as if her heart must break.

HOLLOW SOUNDING AND MYSTERIOUS

There's no replying
To the Wind's sighing,
Telling, foretelling,
Dying, undying,
Dwindling and swelling,
Complaining, droning,
Whistling and moaning,
Ever beginning,
Ending, repeating,
Hinting and dinning,
Lagging and fleeting—
We've no replying
Living or dying
To the Wind's sighing.

What are you telling,
Variable Wind-tone?
What would be teaching,
O sinking, swelling,
Desolate Wind-moan?
Ever for ever
Teaching and preaching,
Never, ah never
Making us wiser —
The earliest riser
Catches no meaning,
The last who hearkens
Garners no gleaning
Of wisdom's treasure,
While the world darkens: —
Living or dying,
In pain, in pleasure,
We've no replying
To wordless flying
Wind's sighing.

A FISHER WIFE

The soonest mended, nothing said;
And help may rise from east or west;
But my two hands are lumps of lead,
My heart sits leaden in my breast.

O north wind swoop not from the north,
O south wind linger in the south,
Oh come not raving raging forth,
To bring my heart into my mouth;

For I've a husband out at sea,
Afloat on feeble planks of wood;
He does not know what fear may be;
I would have told him if I could.

I would have locked him in my arms,
I would have hid him in my heart;
For oh! the waves are fraught with harms,
And he and I so far apart.

WHAT'S IN A NAME?

Why has Spring one syllable less
Than any its fellow season?
There may be some other reason,
And I 'm merely making a guess;
But surely it hoards such wealth
Of happiness, hope and health,
Sunshine and musical sound,
It may spare a foot from its name
Yet all the same
Superabound.

Soft-named Summer,
Most welcome comer,
Brings almost everything
Over which we dream or sing
Or sigh;
But then Summer wends its way,
To-morrow, — to-day, —
Good-bye!

Autumn, — the slow name lingers,
While we likewise flag ;
It silences many singers;
Its slow days drag,
Yet hasten at speed
To leave us in chilly need
For Winter to strip indeed.

In all-lack Winter,
Dull of sense and of sound,
We huddle and shiver
Beside our splinter
Of crackling pine,
Snow in sky and snow on ground.
Winter and cold
Can't last for ever!
To-day, to-morrow, the sun will shine;
When we are old,
But some still are young,
Singing the song
Which others have sung,
Ringing the bells
Which others have rung, —
Even so!
We ourselves, who else?
We ourselves long
Long ago.

MARIANA

Not for me marring or making,
Not for me giving or taking;
I love my Love and he loves not me,
I love my Love and my heart is breaking.

Sweet is Spring in its lovely showing,
Sweet the violet veiled in blowing,
Sweet it is to love and be loved;
Ah, sweet knowledge beyond my knowing!

Who sighs for love sighs but for pleasure,
Who wastes for love hoards up a treasure;
Sweet to be loved and take no count,
Sweet it is to love without measure.

Sweet my Love whom I loved to try for,
Sweet my Love whom I love and sigh for,
Will you once love me and sigh for me,
You my Love whom I love and die for?

BUDS AND BABIES

A million buds are born that never blow,
That sweet with promise lift a pretty head
To blush and wither on a barren bed
And leave no fruit to show.

Sweet, unfulfilled. Yet have I understood
One joy, by their fragility made plain:
Nothing was ever beautiful in vain,
Or all in vain was good.

BOY JOHNNY

"If you'll busk you as a bride
And make ready,
It's I will wed you with a ring,
O fair lady."

"Shall I busk me as a bride,
I so bonny,
For you to wed me with a ring,
O boy Johnny?"

"When you've busked you as a bride
And made ready,
Who else is there to marry you,
O fair lady?"

"I will find my lover out,
I so bonny,
And you shall bear my wedding-train,
O boy Johnny."

LOVE IS STRONG AS DEATH

"I have not sought Thee, I have not found Thee,
I have not thirsted for Thee:
And now cold billows of death surround me,
Buffeting billows of death astound me, —
Wilt Thou look upon, wilt Thou see
Thy perishing me?"

"Yea, I have sought thee, yea, I have found thee,
Yea, I have thirsted for thee,
Yea, long ago with love's bands I bound thee:
Now the Everlasting Arms surround thee, —
Through death's darkness I look and see
And clasp thee to Me."

THE THREAD OF LIFE

The irresponsive silence of the land,
The irresponsive sounding of the sea,
Speak both one message of one sense to me: —
Aloof, aloof, we stand aloof, so stand
Thou too aloof bound with the flawless band
Of inner solitude; we bind not thee;
But who from thy self-chain shall set thee free?
What heart shall touch thy heart?
        what hand thy hand?—
And I am sometimes proud and sometimes meek,
And sometimes I remember days of old
When fellowship seemed not so far to seek
And all the world and I seemed much less cold,
And at the rainbow's foot lay surely gold,
And hope felt strong and life itself not weak.

Thus am I mine own prison. Everything
Around me free and sunny and at ease:
Or if in shadow, in a shade of trees
Which the sun kisses, where the gay birds sing
And where all winds make various murmuring;
Where bees are found, with honey for the bees;
Where sounds are music, and where silences
Are music of an unlike fashioning.
Then gaze I at the merrymaking crew,
And smile a moment and a moment sigh
Thinking: Why can I not rejoice with you?
But soon I put the foolish fancy by:
I am not what I have nor what I do;
But what I was I am, I am even I.

Therefore myself is that one only thing
I hold to use or waste, to keep or give;
My sole possession every day I live,
And still mine own despite Time's winnowing.

Ever mine own, while moons and seasons bring
From crudeness ripeness mellow and sanative;
Ever mine own, till Death shall ply his sieve;
And still mine own, when saints break grave and sing.
And this myself as king unto my King
I give, to Him Who gave Himself for me;
Who gives Himself to me, and bids me sing
A sweet new song of His redeemed set free;
He bids me sing: O death, where is thy sting?
And sing: O grave, where is thy victory?

A HANDY MOLE

A handy Mole who plied no shovel
To excavate his vaulted hovel,
While hard at work met in mid-furrow
An Earthworm boring out his burrow.
Our Mole had dined and must grow thinner
Before he gulped a second dinner,
And on no other terms cared he
To meet a worm of low degree.
The Mole turned on his blindest eye
Passing that base mechanic by;
The Worm entrenched in actual blindness
Ignored or kindness or unkindness;
Each wrought his own exclusive tunnel
To reach his own exclusive funnel.

A plough its flawless track pursuing
Involved them in one common ruin.
Where now the mine and countermine,
The dined-on and the one to dine?
The impartial ploughshare of extinction
Annulled them all without distinction.

A CONTEMPTUOUS FROG

Contemptuous of his home beyond
The village and the village pond,
A large-souled Frog who spurned each byeway,
Hopped along the imperial highway.

Nor grunting pig nor barking dog
Could disconcert so great a frog.
The morning dew was lingering yet
His sides to cool, his tongue to wet;
The night dew when the night should come
A travelled frog would send him home.

Not so, alas! the wayside grass
Sees him no more: — not so, alas!
A broadwheeled wagon unawares
Ran him down, his joys, his cares.
From dying choke one feeble croak
The Frog's perpetual silence broke:
'Ye buoyant Frogs, ye great and small,
Even I am mortal after all.
My road to Fame turns out a wry way:
I perish on this hideous highway, —
Oh for my old familiar byeway!'

The choking Frog sobbed and was gone:
The waggoner strode whistling on.

Unconscious of the carnage done,
Whistling that waggoner strode on,
Whistling (it may have happened so)
"A Froggy would a-wooing go:"
A hypothetic frog trolled he
Obtuse to a reality.

O rich and poor, O great and small,
Such oversights beset us all:
The mangled frog abides incog,
The uninteresting actual frog;
The hypothetic frog alone
Is the one frog we dwell upon.

WHO HAS SEEN THE WIND?

Who has seen the wind?
Neither I nor you.
But when the leaves hang trembling,
The wind is passing through.
Who has seen the wind?
Neither you nor I.
But when the trees bow down their heads,
The wind is passing by.

SLEEPING AT LAST

Sleeping at last, the trouble and tumult over,
Sleeping at last, the struggle and horror past,
Cold and white, out of sight of friend and of lover,
Sleeping at last.

No more a tired heart downcast or overcast,
No more pangs that wring or shifing fears that hover,
Sleeping at last in a dreamless sleep locked fast.

Fast asleep. Singing birds in their leafy cover
Cannot wake her, nor shake her the gusty blast.
Under the purple thyme and the purple clover
Sleeping at last.